G000255279

Reconciliation
The Mercy of Christ

by
Vivian Boland OP

All booklets are published thanks to the
generous support of the members of the
Catholic Truth Society

CATHOLIC TRUTH SOCIETY
PUBLISHERS TO THE HOLY SEE

CONTENTS

1. THE SOUND OF ANGELS CHEERING

Imagine an Olympic stadium packed to capacity on the last day of the games. The marathon is almost over. The crowd waits impatiently for the first runner to enter the stadium. When he or she does there is an explosion of joy and admiration as the crowd shouts its support to help the runner finish the race.

When a sinner repents he or she does so to the sound of angels cheering. It is as if a heavenly stadium were packed with angels who roar their joy and support whenever a sinner appears through the tunnel and limps, however tiredly, towards the finishing line.

The joy of repentance and forgiveness is at the heart of Christian life. It is what Christ has won for us through the mysteries of his life, death and resurrection. The sacrament of baptism is the great celebration of this reality in the Church. The newly baptised dies to sin and is born to a new life. Confirmation brings this life to maturity and it is nourished in the Eucharist. But human beings grow weak in body and in spirit. Where illness threatens their well being, Christ's healing touch reaches them through the sacrament of anointing. Where sin threatens spiritual illness and even death, Christ's forgiveness reaches them through the sacrament of reconciliation.

A culture of no regrets

If the sacrament of reconciliation is a sacrament in crisis as John Paul II has often said, and as pastoral experience seems to bear out, then part of the explanation for this might be that remorse has become practically impossible in our culture.

> *Remorse has become practically impossible in our culture*

The Archbishop of Canterbury, Dr Rowan Williams, writes about this difficulty in his book *Lost Icons: Reflections on Cultural Bereavement* (Edinburgh 2000). One of the virtues we seem to have lost, he argues, is the capacity for remorse (Chapter 3).

If he is right, then the crisis in the sacrament of reconciliation is partly explained by more widespread difficulties about remorse, regret, apology and forgiveness in contemporary experience. The evil in some of the things that have been done in recent history can seem too deep for forgiveness. Who is entitled to forgive people involved in the Holocaust and other genocidal campaigns? What does forgiveness and reconciliation mean in South Africa, the north of Ireland, or after the attacks of September 11th?

The promises of the Bible - 'no need to remember the past', 'behold I make all things new' - can seem incredible in the face of great evil and irreparable loss. It is important to be aware of this background if we want to say something about contrition, reconciliation and forgiveness in a Christian sense, as the New Testament speaks of them.

Forgiveness in the Gospels

Reconciliation is central to the life and work of Jesus, and to the life and work of the Church. But if our capacity to understand and practise remorse has been numbed or otherwise damaged, then our capacity to receive the reconciliation offered by Christ and the Church is also damaged. We are perhaps more like the paralysed man than the Olympic athlete. It may be that we need to be carried into the presence of the forgiving Christ (*Mark* 2:3). It may be that we need to have restored to us the very capacity for accepting and returning forgiveness.

In his teaching and ministry Jesus speaks often about the forgiveness of sins. Most striking is his parable of the prodigal son (*Luke* 15) who is welcomed home by a father prodigal in his love. The father is so generous in forgiving that he does not wait for his son to reach him but sees him approaching from afar, rushes out to meet him and welcomes him home before the son even has time to express his remorse in the speech he had prepared. Jesus tells us that God seeks the sinner just as their owners hunt for a lost coin or a wandering sheep (*Luke* 15).

In his parables Jesus teaches about the generosity and mercy of the Father. In his actions he shows that generosity and mercy in practice. With the woman who anoints his feet, and is famous as a sinner (*Luke* 7), and with the woman caught in the act of adultery (*John* 8), we see the divine generosity and mercy translated into human words and actions. The forgiveness of sins is at the heart of Jesus' work on behalf of Israel and the world. Everybody recognises that his claim to be able to forgive sins is a claim to divine power, for 'who can forgive sins but God alone' (*Mark* 2:7). And yet he interprets his own death as a sacrifice for human salvation. His body is broken that we might be made one. His blood is poured out so that sins might be forgiven. His death on the cross is for the reconciliation of humanity, to put to death the hostility that separates us (*Ephesians* 2:16). 'Through him', we read elsewhere, 'God was pleased to reconcile to himself all things, whether on earth or in heaven, by making peace through the blood of his cross' (*Colossians* 1:20).

Those who seek to follow Christ and to live by his way must be ready to be forgiven and they must be ready

> There will be more joy in heaven over one sinner who repents than over ninety-nine persons who need no repentance. (Luke 15:7).

to forgive. The prayer he teaches his disciples includes 'forgive us our trespasses as we forgive those who trespass against us' (*Matthew* 6:12). Our reconciliation with God cannot be separated from our reconciliation with our fellow human beings with whom we must first be reconciled before bringing our gifts to the altar (*Matthew* 5:23-24).

Forgiveness is not to be miserly or reluctant but generous and free: seventy seven times perhaps, or even seventy times seven (*Matthew* 18). If it lives by this rule, the community of disciples will reverse the pattern of sinful humanity so vividly described in the early chapters of the Bible. As they insisted on a seventy-fold retribution, so the new community seeks to live by a seventy-fold absolution (*Genesis* 4:24). Those cycles or spirals of injustice and revenge that so afflict humanity are broken only by the death of the innocent one who 'offered his back to those who struck him' (*Isaiah* 50:6), who did not return evil for evil (*Romans* 12:17) but asked the Father to forgive those who did not know what they were doing (*Luke* 23:34).

Then Peter went up to him and said, Lord, how often must I forgive my brother if he wrongs me? As often as seven times? Jesus answered, Not seven, I tell you, but seventy-seven times. (Mt 18:21-22).

The Early Church

The Church, the community of His disciples, is given authority and power to continue Christ's work of forgiveness and reconciliation. This is seen in the keys given to Peter with the power to 'bind and loose' (*Matthew* 16:19; 18:18) and it is seen in the breathing of the Spirit on the apostles with the power to 'bind and loose' (*John* 20:23). From the earliest times Christians recognised the link between their own experience of forgiveness and their task of bringing others to the same joy. 'It was while we were still sinners that Christ died for us' (*Romans* 5:8-9). 'Through Christ we have now received reconciliation' (*Romans* 5:11). 'Her sins, which were many, have been forgiven; hence she has shown great love' (*Luke* 7:47).

When people ask what they are supposed to do in response to hearing the gospel proclaimed, the answer is that they are to repent and be baptised in the name of Jesus Christ so that their sins might be forgiven and they might receive the gift of the Holy Spirit (*Acts* 2:37-38). 'Confess your sins to one another', James reminds his readers (*James* 5:16). The reconciled become ambassadors of reconciliation:

...if anyone is in Christ, there is a new creation: everything old has passed away; see, everything has become new! All this is from God, who reconciled us to himself through

Christ, and has given us the ministry of reconciliation; that is, in Christ God was reconciling the world to himself, not counting their trespasses against them, and entrusting the message of reconciliation to us. So we are ambassadors for Christ, since God is making his appeal through us: we entreat you on behalf of Christ, be reconciled to God. For our sake he made him to be sin who knew no sin, so that in him we might become the righteousness of God. (2 Corinthians 5:17-21).

The forgiveness and reconciliation preached by Christ and established in his paschal mystery, reach us through Baptism and the Eucharist in the first place. The 'new creation', our participation in the life of God who is love, comes about through our baptism in the name of the Father and of the Son and of the Holy Spirit. The 'new life' we receive in Baptism is sustained through our celebration of the Eucharistic mysteries in which the Father is praised with the gift of his own Son through the working of the Holy Spirit.

The missions of the Son and the Spirit are with a view to reconciling the world to God. We can describe them as the arms of the Father, with which he reaches out to draw the world to Himself, bringing it into relationship with Him by rescuing it from the power of evil, death and sin, and so establishing it securely in His peace. For the Christian tradition this is what happens with the sending of Christ and the Spirit and it is what continues to happen through the Church, the community of Christ's disciples who continue to make him present through its life of worshipping God and serving humanity.

When the Church celebrates reconciliation the Father receives the repentant child who comes back to him, Christ places the lost sheep on his shoulders to bring it back to the sheepfold, and the Holy Spirit sanctifies the temple of God again and comes to dwell more fully within it. To be reconciled with God means also to be reconciled with the Church, specifically to return to participation in the Eucharist. It may even be that those whom the community has felt obliged to keep at a distance (*1 Corinthians* 5:1-5; *2 Corinthians* 2:5-11) are, by the power of God's Spirit, restored to full communion. The Church's discipline of penance, although it has taken different forms at different times, has always had this as its goal, the great joy at the banquet of Christ's church over the sinner who returns from afar.

2. DRAMAS OF SIN AND REPENTANCE

From the beginning the Church realised that the mysteries entrusted to it by Christ and the Spirit included the authority and power to reconcile sinners who had already been baptised. The sacramental life of the Christian community included not only the great sacraments of Baptism and the Eucharist, celebrated at the Lord's explicit command and in memory of him, but others too that were relevant to crucial experiences and responsibilities of the Christian life and that were understood to originate in the ministry and paschal work of Christ and so to have been instituted by Him.

The experiences of illness and sin were to be touched by the Church's ministry

Specifically, the experiences of illness and sin were to be touched by the Church's ministry as the sick and the sinful had been sought out, touched and healed by Christ. The responsibilities of marriage and priesthood were callings to which God's grace summoned individual Christians on behalf of the community. These two responsibilities were understood as essential to the Church's life - without them the Church is not fully present - and so are understood also to be sacraments of the Church.

Christians who, through sin, had fallen away from the new life they received in baptism could be reconciled with God and the Church through a special sacrament called 'reconciliation'. It is also called the sacrament of 'penance' because of the Christian virtue with which it is most closely associated. This sacrament is the most important element in the practice of that virtue. In many places it is known simply as 'confession' from the central action undertaken by the repentant Christian, namely the verbal acknowledgement of God's mercy and of his or her own sinfulness.

The Gelasian Sacramentary, a text from the 6th century that may include even earlier material, contains a prayer which refers to confession (*confessio*) and which prays that the penitent may be admitted to the sacrament of reconciliation (*ad sacramentum reconciliationis*). This is the name by which the sacrament is now properly known, although 'penance' and 'confession' may still be used.

Forgiveness after Baptism

There are some texts in the New Testament that seem to exclude the possibility of a new repentance where a person has been baptised and then falls into serious sin. The most severe teaching about this is found in the Letter to the Hebrews. In chapter 6 of that letter we read:

As for those people who were once brought into the light, and tasted the gift from heaven, and received a share of the Holy Spirit, and appreciated the good message of God and the powers of the world to come, and yet in spite of this have fallen away - it is impossible for them to be renewed a second time. They cannot be repentant if they have wilfully crucified the Son of God and openly mocked him. (Hebrews 6:4-8).

Similarly rigorous teaching is found in Hebrews 10 - 'if, after we have been given knowledge of the truth, we should deliberately commit any sins, then there is no longer any sacrifice for them' (10:26) - and again in Hebrews 12 which compares the Christian who falls away from the faith with Esau who lost his chance to be blessed and was subsequently rejected even though he pleaded with tears (12:14-17).

Saint Paul also speaks in a severe way about the situation of some sinful Christians: see 1 Corinthians 5:3-5; 2 Corinthians 2:6-11 and 1 Timothy 1:18-20. We should recall also those passages in the gospels where Jesus speaks of a sin against the Holy Spirit that cannot be forgiven (*Matthew* 12:32 and *Luke* 12:10). The Gospel of Mark says that this sin of blasphemy against the Holy Spirit is 'an eternal sin' (*Mark* 3:29).

From such texts we learn many things. We learn that there is a danger of under-estimating the seriousness of the decisions to which the Christian faith calls us. We learn that there is a danger of presumption in relation to God's grace and the promise of salvation. It is true that despair is a sin against the virtue of hope but so too is presumption. Just as we ought not to give up because of our sins, neither ought we to sit back and assume that they are of no account. Those who grow in holiness, as they come to know God better also come to know sin better. The saints are more rather than less sensitive to the reality of sin not because of the likely punishments it might earn for us but because they see more clearly the kind of offence it is against God's goodness and love. The saints understand the sadness and tragedy of sin better than sinners.

The Sacrament in the Early Church

In practice, though, the Church developed a discipline of penance that allowed for the re-admission of baptised Christians who had fallen into grave sin. It came to understand the texts quoted above as referring to an explicit denial or rejection of mercy and grace, an explicit refusal of forgiveness. The sin that excludes a person permanently from the presence of God will be a form of despair that refuses to accept the blessing of God's forgiving presence. This is what we mean by hell: a self-chosen exclusion from the love of God. We pray and hope that no human person will end in that state, but we do not know.

The Church accepted, then, from the earliest times, that it did indeed have the authority and power to reconcile sinners with God not only through the sacrament of baptism but through another sacrament intended for baptised persons who had fallen into serious sin. The really serious sins that broke communion with

> *The really serious sins that broke communion with the Church were murder, adultery and apostasy*

the Church were murder, adultery and apostasy. The implications and consequences of such actions were as obvious then as they are now. There was also the decision of the 'Council of Jerusalem' that identified these as things Christians ought not to do (*Acts* 15:20; 15:29).

But even in the event of such sins there was the hope of reconciliation. In the early centuries the process of reconciling sinners with the Church had two striking features: it could be undertaken only once, and it was a process conducted in public. In a famous image Tertullian, a North African writer, speaks of reconciliation as 'a second plank after shipwreck'. This second plank can, however, only be offered once. Hermas, Ephrem and others of the early teachers of the Church speak about a 'second-class salvation' that is possible for the baptised who have failed to persevere in the commitment they have undertaken. Saint John Climacus, who died in 649, says that repentance is the renewal of Baptism and a contract with God for a second life.

Penitence

Penance and reconciliation was public in these early centuries and sinners were obliged to identify themselves as such before the community. But this does not mean that they had to confess their sins publicly. The bishop would know their sins, presumably, at least from the time of Cyprian of Carthage who made confession part of the rite. In Rome Pope Leo I makes it clear that public confession of sins is not required although there seems to be some confusion about whether he went on to praise it where it was freely chosen as an act of humility or to condemn it as something that should not be done. The important thing is that penance and reconciliation were public even where confession was not. The sacrament of reconciliation referred, then, to the formal conclusion of the process by which penitents were restored to the communion of the Church by the bishop.

The distinction between penance as a Christian virtue, and the sacrament of penance or reconciliation, is also clear from early times. The call to repentance is extended to all and conversion is not just a once off experience but a daily task for the believer. The liturgical celebration of Lent made this very clear, an annual recalling of the evangelical summons to *metanoia,* a change of heart and mind. The virtue of penitence or penance was practised through prayer, almsgiving, other works of service, and various kinds of mortification and self-denial. Fidelity to the gospel required a disciplined life and discipline presupposed some ascetical practices to keep the mind and heart focused on God and on our need for God. If the Christian was an

> *The virtue of penitence or penance was practised through prayer, almsgiving and self-denial*

athlete then he needed to stay fit for the struggle against evil. This essential aspect of Christian living was celebrated in the liturgies of the Church, in particular in the Eucharist, Baptism and what came to be called the Sacrament of Reconciliation.

Frequent Confession

At about the beginning of the 7th century there is a change. The discipline of once in a lifetime and public penance and reconciliation is replaced by the practice of frequent and private penance and reconciliation. This change came about largely through the influence of monks in Celtic lands. It emerged from their practice of spiritual direction in which they checked in now and again with a spiritual father and spoke with this teacher or guide about the difficulties they were experiencing in living according to the gospel. Christians are obliged to correct one another, to encourage one another, and to bear one another's burdens. It is part of what is involved in loving one another. The monks did this for each other and from this spiritual accompaniment emerged the sacrament of reconciliation in something more like the form we recognise today.

The development that took place with what are called the penitential books of the Celtic churches is generally regarded as a good thing. It took away the humiliation attached to public penance. It established the idea that this sacrament is one to which people might have recourse more than once. It also established the idea that this sacrament is one to which people might have recourse even when they have not fallen into serious sin. Here is a help, more than that, a sacramental help, for the ordinary difficulties and weaknesses of Christian living as well as for reconciliation in the event of serious sin. Like the earlier Christians, the monks understood penitence to be both a virtue and a sacrament just as they continued to use the terms 'penance' (*paenitentia*) and 'reconciliation' (*reconciliatio*).

This form of celebrating the sacrament is called auricular confession. It involved a one to one confession by the penitent into the ear (*auricula*) of a priest. Some see this development as positive while others believe it had negative consequences. The penitential books included extensive lists of sins, distinguished according to the circumstances in which they were committed. They were also concerned with the frequency with which these particular sins were committed. When many centuries later the Council of Trent decreed that sins were to be confessed 'according to species and number', this concern with full or integral confession had its roots in the penitential books. Some believe that the development of auricular confession tended to encourage anxiety, even scrupulosity, about the minute details of behaviour (thoughts, words, actions) to the neglect of more general attitudes and dispositions. People might forget that omission - what we neglected to do - can also be sinful.

Penance

The fact that tariffs had to be imposed by the confessor - punishments to fit the crime, as it were - was another reason why it was necessary to identify the species of the sin and to report its frequency. This is the origin of what we know as the 'penance' assigned by the priest in the sacrament. While there are very good reasons for such penances, as we shall see, it could happen that people might begin to think that they had 'paid' for their sin and that some kind of commercial transaction was involved in this sacrament. 'How much did you get?', we often asked each other as children after we had been to confession. Misunderstandings of what is involved in sin can follow from this, and sometimes did, but this is not a good reason for ignoring the good things that the new practice of the sacrament involved.

Through the Middle Ages there continues to be diversity in the penitential liturgies of the Church. The virtue and the sacrament continue to be connected. Monks are 'penitents' who spend their whole lives trying to develop this virtue and to be converted to Christ. Spiritual direction and guidance remain closely associated with the sacrament of reconciliation although this need not necessarily be so. The confession by nuns to their 'spiritual mother' and of other Christians to lay directors is not unknown in the Middle Ages.

The next important moment in the development of the sacrament is at the Fourth Lateran Council in 1215. This Council solidified the ritual of reconciliation as developed by the Celtic monks. At the same time it maintained the link between the sacrament and the reconciliation of the serious sinner by insisting that all Christians who were conscious of serious sin must celebrate this sacrament each year. This continues to be the law of the Church for its members:

All the faithful who have reached the age of discretion are bound faithfully to confess their grave sins at least once a year (Code of Canon Law 989).

A little later Thomas Aquinas explained that confession to God is obligatory under natural law - all human beings will tend to want to do it - whereas confession to a man - that is to a priest in the sacrament - is obligatory by divine law.

One might argue that the earlier, public ritual of penance with its order of penitents and communal celebration of reconciliation was more straightforwardly sacramental in the sense that people's separation from the Church and their being received back were visibly expressed in a more striking and obvious way. On the other hand many feel that the development from a sacrament that could be celebrated only once in a lifetime to one that can be received again and again outweighs any other losses there might have been. In any case the latest renewal of the sacrament, after Vatican II, sought to restore to its celebration something of the communal character of the earlier rites. It is to that latest renewal that we now turn.

The New Rite of Reconciliation

The Second Vatican Council (1962-1965) called for a renewal of the rite of penance and reconciliation. Its rituals and prayers were to be reviewed in such a way that the nature and effects of the sacrament would be more clearly expressed (*Constitution on the Sacred Liturgy*, paragraph 72). The new rite was published in 1973. A short Liturgy of the Word was placed at the beginning of each celebration of the sacrament whether communal or individual. The new rite sought to combine the values of the earlier tradition of public penance and reconciliation with those of the later tradition of individual and private penance and reconciliation. So the communal aspect of sin is stressed along with its social consequences. The rite allows for communal celebrations of penance and reconciliation. At the same time individual confession and absolution remains the ordinary way of celebrating the sacrament. The ancient name was restored so that it is now officially known as 'the sacrament of reconciliation'.

There are three forms of this new rite of reconciliation. The first is for the reconciliation of individual penitents. The second is for the reconciliation of several penitents with individual confession and absolution. The third is for the reconciliation of penitents with general confession and absolution. This latter is a form of the rite that can be used only in exceptional cases. In spite of the general decline in the use of the sacrament in some countries, the Church continues to insist on the central importance of individual confession and absolution. We will consider why this one to one confession and absolution is so highly valued by the Church that it is regarded as the 'normal' or 'typical' celebration of the sacrament, one that ought to be made available to Catholics in all but the most exceptional of circumstances.

Individual Confession

At the heart of this sacrament, in its ordinary celebration, is an encounter between two human beings. From this certain things follow, a set of issues concerned with what John Paul II has called 'the methodology of dialogue' (*Reconciliatio et Paenitentia* 29). This particular encounter of two human beings is ecclesial. One of the human beings involved is a priest and is not therefore present in a personal capacity. His relationship with Christ and with the church entitles him to be present in the role he has here. The other person involved is a sinner and must be a contrite sinner if he or she is to fulfil the role he or she has here. Of course the one who is a priest in one celebration of this sacrament will be the sinner in another celebration of it, when the priest himself becomes the penitent.

The term 'role' is used deliberately in the preceding paragraph, not to trivialise the nature of this encounter in the sacrament of reconciliation but to bring out that it is a dramatic enactment of a mystery of salvation. This human, ecclesial encounter is sacramental and that means it is also liturgical. The sacraments are not just holy things but are sacred rites. When we speak about a 'rite' we are speaking about a liturgy of the Church, a celebration in which the community of disciples is gathered, or at least represented. Certain things follow from the fact that these rites are sacramental and certain things follow from the fact that they are liturgical.

As a sacramental liturgy of the Church it is a particular way of being in the presence of the Risen Lord. Christ is always present among His people to bring them to the fullness of life that He has promised. In the sacrament of reconciliation we meet Him as the Christ who forgives and strengthens us. He opens for us again the way to the Father and renews in us the gift of his Spirit. As a sacramental liturgy it involves words, gestures, texts, bodily dispositions, perhaps music and singing and silence, physical actions that signify spiritual realities.

> *In the sacrament of reconciliation we meet Him as the Christ who forgives and strengthens us*

We must consider all this at greater length. Suffice it to conclude this chapter by repeating that what is required for the celebration of the sacrament of reconciliation is a sinner who is contrite, ready to confess and ready to do penance, and a priest from whom the sinner will receive encouragement, guidance and absolution. In the words and gestures exchanged in this encounter the sacrament is completed. We can usefully meditate, then, on what it takes to be a good sinner (meaning one ready for the celebration of this sacrament) and what it takes to be a good confessor (meaning one ready for the celebration of this sacrament). We must consider the virtues or qualities of the good sinner and the virtues or qualities of the good confessor. There is no better way of doing this than by considering what it is they must do in the celebration of the sacrament: what is meant by contrition and confession, by absolution and penance.

3. THE GOOD SINNER

At the heart of the sacrament of reconciliation is the encounter between a sinner and a priest. For the purposes of celebrating this sacrament a 'good' sinner and a 'good' confessor are required. The good sinner is one who is contrite, confesses his sins, intends not to sin again, and undertakes some penance or 'satisfaction' as a way of completing the sacramental celebration.

Contrition

We can say that the matter required for the sacrament of reconciliation is a sinner. Those who have no need of repentance have no need for this sacrament. This sinner - to be more precise - is a contrite sinner, one who seeks to turn away from sin and hear again the good news of redemption. For the celebration of the sacrament, then, the sinner's contribution is sins and contrition. To be contrite means to be sorry for the sins about to be confessed. In order to be genuine, contrition must be accompanied by a purpose of amendment. This means a firm intention not to commit the same sins again. It seems reasonable that this should be so: if I am genuinely sorry about a particular way of behaving or about something I have done or have failed to do, then I will want to be free of it in the future.

Much has been written about 'contrition' and those who received catechetical instruction at an earlier period will have had the difference between imperfect and perfect contrition explained to them. The 'act of perfect contrition' is an elusive thing. It means that we are contrite - sorry - about our sins for no reason other than the offence those sins offer to the love and goodness of God. Imperfect contrition (sometimes called attrition) means sorrow for our sins for some reason less than the love of God: because we fear the punishments that come with sinning, for example. Part of the 'preferential bias for the sinner' that has guided the development of the sacrament is the Church's acceptance that imperfect contrition is sufficient for the celebration of reconciliation.

The reason for this acceptance is because the Church knows that 'perfect contrition' is a gift of God's grace and not something we can generate from within our own resources. Imperfect contrition means we are turning back towards home, beginning the journey back to reconciliation with God. It was a combination of ordinary deprivation and

Scholastic theologians analysed sacraments in terms of matter and form . The matter is the visible element or symbolic gesture, such as anointing with oil. The form is the actual words or prayer used, which brings out the significance of and makes explicit what is already there.

disillusionment that brought the prodigal son to his senses and made him think of returning home (*Luke* 15:14-19). God continues to use ordinary events and our responses to them to sow the seeds of contrition in our hearts. Even a sense of humiliation, failure or embarrassment is enough to generate imperfect contrition and from that perfect contrition may be born.

> *God continues to use ordinary events and our responses to them to sow the seeds of contrition in our hearts*

The contrite sinner is expected then to make a good confession. This means as full a confession of serious sins as is humanly possible. In preparation for the sacrament of reconciliation we are asked to 'call to mind our sins' and to do it at much greater length than we do at the beginning of Mass. We are asked to remember. For Saint John of the Cross memory is the seat of hope. Hope is born in memory and flourishes with remembrance. This is a very interesting link and very relevant for this sacrament.

In speaking as he does about memory, John of the Cross stands in a long tradition. Many philosophers and theologians had already written about this theme. John of the Cross used a division of the powers of the soul that he learned from Saint Augustine of Hippo. For Augustine the essential powers or capacities of the human being are mind, memory and will. In his work

The Ascent of Mount Carmel, John of the Cross then placed the central Christian virtues of faith, hope and charity within these powers of the human soul. Faith is the best possible use of the mind, hope is the best possible use of the memory and charity is the best possible use of the will.

The Importance of Remembering

The pre-Christian Greek philosopher Aristotle had many interesting things to say about remembering and so too did the pre-Christian Roman philosopher Cicero. Aristotle distinguished memory and reminiscence, meaning by memory those things that are immediately present to our minds and by reminiscence those things that can be brought back to mind because they are associated or linked with the things we remember more easily. For Cicero memory is part of the virtue of prudence. To be prudent is to have a kind of over-view of our life and its direction, to keep our purpose in mind as we go about our business from day to day. Memory is important if we are to learn from experience because memory is the knowledge of past things. We could not really talk about experience if we did not have the capacity for remembering.

Saint Thomas Aquinas later used what he learned from Aristotle and Cicero in speaking about the Christian life. He agrees with Aristotle that there are things we remember easily and others that are not at first remembered but that can be brought back to mind because of their association with the things we do remember more easily. From Cicero he accepted that memory is part of prudence. Our understanding of the varied situations and

> *Good remembering of the past is essential for wise counsel about the future*

circumstances of life, says Saint Thomas, is only gained through experience in which memory plays a key role. He writes a short 'guide to good remembering' in which he says that we remember best the things that cause us anxiety and the things that excite our love. Good remembering of the past is essential for wise counsel about the future.

There is great wisdom then in the Church's invitation to 'call to mind our sins', particularly with a view to celebrating the sacrament of reconciliation.

The English word 'remember' is sometimes understood as the opposite of 'dismember'. What has been broken up needs to be put back together. It is one way of thinking about reconciliation. Relationships that have been disrupted and fragmented are healed and restored so that what had become broken into bits and pieces, is once again a unity. The narrative of our lives, disrupted by sin, is once again on track. In both Latin and Greek to remember means to be mindful. A certain kind of mindfulness is asked of the contrite sinner.

In modern times the practices of counselling and psychotherapy are particularly concerned with remembering. They seek to bring healing through good remembering. These practices have added further to our understanding of memory, in particular by stressing that certain memories carry a powerful emotional charge and that this sometimes leads to us choosing to bury some memories. From the point of view of celebrating the sacrament of reconciliation it is enough to recognise that some memories are difficult to bear just as some memories are difficult to share.

Remembering the Old Testament

It is not only philosophers and psychologists who have written about memory. The Jewish and Christian scriptures also speak about the importance of remembering, of keeping things in mind and calling things to mind. *Anamnesis* or remembrance is a central theme in the Bible. The people are invited to remember moments and aspects of the relationship between them and God especially the great deeds of God on their behalf. The creed of Israel, the great *Shema Yisrael*, requires believers to 'keep', 'recite', 'talk about', 'bind', 'fix' and 'write' the words of the Torah (*Deuteronomy* 6:4-9). They are to take care not to forget (*Deuteronomy* 6:12) and must remember to observe the commandments of God (*Numbers* 15:39f).

The great intervention of God on behalf of the people is in the plagues of Egypt, the slaying of the first-born and the escape of the Hebrews from Egypt across the Red Sea and into the wilderness. The feast that celebrates this liberation, Passover, is to be 'a day of remembrance' for the people forever (*Exodus* 12:14). They are to remember what God did for them on that day (*Exodus* 13:3; *Deuteronomy* 11:2). They are to remember all that the Lord their God has done for them in 'the days of old and the years long past' (*Deuteronomy* 32:7).

But it is not only the people who remember God. It is also that God who is faithful remembers the people (*Genesis* 9:15; *Isaiah* 49:15). Moses asks God, when he is tempted to reject the people, to remember his earlier promises to Abraham, Isaac and Jacob (*Exodus* 32:13; *Deuteronomy* 9:27). God does remember them as he remembers also the land promised to them and to their descendants (*Leviticus* 26:42, 45). Individual members of God's people ask God to remember them in moments of difficulty and danger: for example Samson (Judges 16:28), Hannah (*1 Samuel* 1:11), Esther (Esther 14:12) and Hezekiah (*2 Kings* 20:3; *Isaiah* 38:3).

Solomon in his prayer asks God to remember the covenant He made with his servant David, Solomon's father (*2 Chronicles* 6:42). The psalms frequently ask God to remember his people's offerings (*Psalm* 20:3), to remember his own goodness rather than their sins (*Psalms* 25:7; 79:8), to remember that they are his people (*Psalm* 74:2). In return they promise to remember God and his great actions on their behalf (*Psalm* 42:4, 6).

They will remember his wonders of old (*Psalm* 77:11), his works, miracles and judgements (*Psalms* 105:5; 143:5).

> *The psalms ask God to remember his own goodness rather than the people's sins*

To the Jewish people in exile in Babylon God promises not to remember their sins but to do a new thing on their behalf (*Isaiah* 43:18). Jeremiah asks God to remember and not to break his covenant with them (*Jeremiah* 14:21). The new covenant of which Jeremiah speaks is one in which God will forgive his people and remember their sin no more (*Jeremiah* 31:34; *Hebrews* 8:12). The covenant is re-established through a mutual remembering, of the people by God and of God by the people (*Ezekiel* 16:60-63). Where such things are not remembered then the punishments of sin inevitably follow (*Isaiah* 46:8; *Ezekiel* 20:43; 36:31; *Hosea* 8:13; 9:9).

The exiles returning to Jerusalem are encouraged to 'remember the Lord who is great and awesome', and they re-establish their life as a people on the strength of that memory (*Nehemiah* 4:14). They ask God to 'remember mercy' (*Habakkuk* 3:2) and they promise to remember God's law (*Malachi* 4:4). It is not just the people who are to remember God and his deeds. It is just as likely that it is God who is asked to remember and the people place their hopes on the fact that God does remember them.

Remembering the New Testament

This rich sense of remembering continues in the New Testament and in the Church's liturgies. Zechariah, the father of John the Baptist, sees in the birth of his son a sign that God has remembered his mercy (*Luke* 1:54). The disciples are to remember that Christ is with them to the end of the age (*Matthew* 28:20). The prayer of the good thief has become a prayer for every Christian: 'Jesus, remember me when you come into your kingdom' (*Luke* 23:42). The disciples need to remember what Jesus has taught them (*Luke* 24:6; *John* 15:20; 16:4; *2 Peter* 3:2). To believe is to remember Jesus Christ who has risen from the dead (*2 Timothy* 2:8).

Above all the bread and cup of the Eucharist are blessed and shared as a memorial of him (*Luke* 22:19; *1 Corinthians* 11:23-27). This refers not to an historical memory, back through chronological time as it were, but to a liturgical and sacramental remembering in which, in the presence of the Father, we 'remind' Him of Christ and of his sacrifice that has taken away our sins. The Eucharist is the great act of remembering undertaken by the Church and the sacrament of reconciliation is connected with it.

To celebrate reconciliation is to remember our sins and our need for forgiveness. It is also to remember Jesus the Lamb of God who takes away the sins of the world. It is to remember God, the Father of Jesus and our Father also, who does not desire the death of the sinner but rather that he should turn from his sins and live (*Ezekiel* 18:23). We are to think of ourselves as dead to sin but alive for God in Christ Jesus (*Romans* 6:11).

The Examination of Conscience

Part of the preparation for the celebration of reconciliation is the examination of our conscience. This means engaging in some 'good remembering' in order to celebrate the sacrament well. Conscience will normally tell us very quickly what our sins are. It is relatively easy to remember serious wrongs we have done and serious omissions. In the ancient world conscience was connected particularly with the sense of guilt. The term 'guilt' can frighten people and it is true that there are ways in which people can be afflicted by inappropriate or disproportionate guilt. At the same time it is part of being a mature human being that we have a keen awareness or sensitivity about what we have done wrong.

The examination of conscience is enriched by the deeper sense of remembering spoken of above. We are to remember our sins, yes, but also God's law, God's mercy, the great things God has done on behalf of the people.

Above all we are to remember Jesus Christ and his sacrifice for our sins, our Saviour 'who wants all to be saved and to come to the knowledge of the truth' (*1 Timothy* 2:4).

> *...it is part of being a mature human being that we have a keen awareness or sensitivity about what we have done wrong*

There are some obstacles to good remembering. Psychology recognises that some events can be so traumatic that our memory of them disappears from consciousness and is only recovered with difficulty. For its part the Bible recognises 'hidden faults', sins to which we remain blind but of which we may become aware through the preaching of the gospel and the guidance of others (*Psalm* 19:6; *Isaiah* 43:8; 56:10; *Matthew* 13:13; *Revelation* 3:17 and *John* 9:40-41). The painful experience of growth towards moral and spiritual maturity will always involve a growing awareness of these 'blind spots' in our character and behaviour.

There are difficulties about remembering some things and there may also be difficulties about recounting what we do remember to someone else. We are asked to do both in celebrating the sacrament, not just to call our sins to mind but to confess them to the priest. There may be natural feelings of embarrassment accompanying the memory of our sins. Our thoughts, words, deeds and omissions may seem petty, sordid, infantile, perverse, unjust, unworthy, and so on. Such feelings may be difficult to bear even in the anonymity of the confessional.

The traditions of confessional practice in the Church recognise that there may be situations where physical or moral impossibility excuses a person from individual and integral confession. Physical impossibility seems clear enough - you are trekking to the North Pole or sailing across the Pacific Ocean and the nearest priest is hundreds of miles away. Moral impossibility arises where, for example, the only priest available to hear your confession is someone to whom, for good reasons, you ought not to confess. The priest puts his name on the confessional so that you know who he is even if he does not know who you are. Embarrassment alone is not sufficient for moral impossibility in regard to confessing one's sins but it is important to know that such situations may arise.

Our remembering in preparation for the sacrament is nothing like the painful process of Freudian psychoanalysis but simply a calling to mind of our sins as well as we can at the particular moment in which we celebrate the sacrament. We will, please God, have other opportunities and we may remember other things then. At the same time we need to accept that there may be faults still hidden from us, selfish and unjust ways of behaving of which we are not aware. But life itself is normally enough to bring these things home to us eventually if we remain open to God in prayer and to our neighbour in kindness.

People use different methods in examining their consciences. One is to recall the Ten Commandments, or the two great commandments to love God and to love our neighbour, and to compare our lives with these. It can also be done by thinking about the theological virtues of faith, hope and charity and the cardinal virtues of justice, temperance, fortitude and prudence. Or it can be done by reflecting on one's fundamental choices and commitments, the duties specific to one's state in life.

The Confession of Sins

At the heart of the celebration of reconciliation is the encounter between two human beings, sinner and priest. This encounter takes the form of a conversation or verbal exchange whose subject matter is sin and forgiveness. As we have seen, there are forms of celebrating the sacrament that do not involve this one to one encounter but these are for exceptional circumstances. The normal way in which the sacrament is celebrated is with individual confession to a priest and individual absolution from him.

The Church has continued to insist that there is something of great value for the sacrament in this one-to-one encounter. This has been repeated most recently in the Apostolic Letter *Misericordia Dei* of John Paul II, issued in April 2002, in which he says that this ordering of the sacrament is, as the Council of Trent had said, 'by divine decree'. The Pope writes:

The church has always seen an essential link between the judgement entrusted to the priest in the Sacrament and the need for penitents to name their own sins, except where this is not possible. Since, therefore, the integral confession of serious sins is by divine decree a constitutive part of the Sacrament, it is in no way subject to the discretion of pastors (dispensation, interpretation, local customs, etc.). In the relevant disciplinary norms, the competent ecclesiastical authority merely indicates the criteria for distinguishing a real impossibility of confessing one s sins from other situations in which the impossibility is only apparent or can be surmounted. (Misericordia Dei, April 2002).

Theology, accepting that the sacrament may on occasion be celebrated in other ways, will nevertheless try to see what is fitting or appropriate about the elements of its normal celebration. There are many encounters to which one might allude that are more or less analogous to that of the sinner and the priest. Friends or lovers talk in order to understand how they have hurt one another and how they might find healing and forgiveness. Parent and child reason together about behaviour and attitudes, whether they are right or wrong, good or bad. Teacher and student work together towards improvement and development. Closer analogies might be the conversation between a spiritual guide and the person seeking guidance, or the conversation between fellow Christians seeking to encourage one another in faith and to call each other to a more generous living of it. We have seen that the practice of individual, auricular confession emerged from the traditions of spiritual accompaniment and encouragement among the Celtic monks.

It has sometimes been suggested that the encounter of counsellor and client, or therapist and patient, is comparable to that of priest and penitent. It has even been claimed that in modern times these latter relationships have, for many people, replaced the encounter in the sacrament of reconciliation.

Whatever about these analogies, the meeting between sinner and confessor in the sacrament of reconciliation is unique precisely in the fact of its being a sacrament of the Church. It is an encounter and exchange between human beings that forms part of a particular symbolic universe. It involves not only the two individuals visibly participating in the exchange but also Christ and therefore also the Church. The forgiveness hoped for is not just a grace recalled or anticipated but is a grace given in the moment of absolution itself. Even the most gifted of counsellors and therapists will not claim to absolve people of their sins.

The sinner is required then to confess his or her sins. Confess is an important term in Christian history and not only because for a long time it provided the name for this sacrament. The confessor is primarily the one who bears public witness to the goodness and mercy of God. It is part of the dignity of the sinner that in celebrating this sacrament, a public liturgy of the Church celebrated in a public if confidential way, he is confessing the faith and declaring before the Church his belief in God and in God's mercy. We can say that the confessing sinner is also a confessor, in its other pronunciation, in other words a confessor of the faith.

> *Even the most gifted of counsellors and therapists will not claim to absolve people of their sins*

The Bible provides us with many examples of the power of confession and the two meanings, of confessing one's sins and confessing God's greatness, are often linked (*1 Kings* 8:33-35; *Joshua* 7:19; *Ezra* 10:1, 11; *Nehemiah* 1:6; 9:3; *Daniel* 9:20). John the Baptist calls on the people to repent and to turn again to God by confessing their sins and being baptised (*Matthew* 3:6; *Mark* 1:5). Both senses of confession continue to be linked in the New Testament (*Romans* 15:9; *1 John* 1:9) while the Letter to the Hebrews refers to the faith itself, the Christian way, as 'our confession' (*Hebrews* 3:1; 4:14; 10:23). The Letter of James encourages the disciples to confess their sins to one another and to pray for one another so that they may be healed (*James* 5:16 and see also *Galatians* 6:1-2 and *Matthew* 18:15-20).

The confession of sins must be 'integral' according to the teaching of the Church. Serious sins must be confessed according to species (what did you do / not do?) and number (how many times?). Why is this? We saw how the practice originated in the tariffs recommended in the penitential books for different kinds of sinful behaviour. The person hearing the confession needed to know what had been done and how often it had been done if they were to make a fair judgement about the tariff or penance to be imposed.

While this insistence on integral confession can be seen negatively, and has often been experienced negatively, it is important to try to understand it positively. To name something is to make it really present just as to remember a name is to bring alive the person who is named. It is not only psychological health that is served by people actually articulating things, 'getting them out', getting things 'off their chest', naming them and so bringing them from the inside to the outside. Above all the Church insists on the essential character of the integral confession of sins because that dialogue between the sinner and the priest is the natural human basis or visible matter of the sacrament. That dialogue or exchange is the effective sign of spiritual realities. This exchange between two human beings becomes an exchange between the sinner and Christ, in Christ's body the Church.

In paragraph 31 of the post-synodal exhortation *Reconciliatio et Paenitentia* (1984) John Paul II wrote about the significance of the act of confessing:

The confession of sins is required, first of all, because the sinner must be known by the person who in the sacrament exercises the role of judge. He has to evaluate both the seriousness of the sins and the repentance of the penitent; he also exercises the role of healer, and must acquaint himself with the condition of the sick person in order to treat and heal him. But the individual confession also has the value of a sign: a sign of the meeting of the sinner with the mediation of the Church in the person of the minister; a sign of the person s revealing of self as a sinner in the sight of God and the Church, of facing his own sinful condition in the eyes of God.

The confession of sins therefore cannot be reduced to a mere attempt at psychological self-liberation, even though it corresponds to that legitimate and natural need, inherent in the human heart, to open oneself to another. It is a liturgical act, solemn in its dramatic nature, yet humble and sober in the grandeur of its meaning. It is the act of the Prodigal Son who returns to his Father and is welcomed by him with the kiss of peace. It is an act of honesty and courage. It is an act of entrusting oneself, beyond sin, to the mercy that forgives.

Thus we understand why the confession of sins must ordinarily be individual and not collective, just as sin is a deeply personal matter. But at the same time this confession in a way forces sin out of the secret of the heart and thus out of the area of pure individuality, emphasising its social character as well, for through the minister of Penance it is the ecclesial community, which has been wounded by sin, that welcomes anew the repentant and forgiven sinner.

Nowhere else perhaps is human action valued more highly than in Catholic Christianity. Whatever we think, say, do, or omit serves to dispose us in the direction of goodness or away from it. It is not just behaviour, it is action that the Church values. We behave all the time but we do not always act in properly human ways. As with other creatures the behaviour of humans can be studied and analysed by scientists of various disciplines. But action is specifically human because it originates in the one who is acting, is done with awareness, and is done freely. Even sinful human action - which is radically inhuman in one sense - testifies to the dignity of our having been made in the image and likeness of God .

The value placed by the Church on the integral confession of sins is thus a way in which it honours and respects the dignity of each human individual, the fact that we are created in the image and likeness of God, with understanding, freedom and creative power. The fact that the context of this recognition in the sacrament of reconciliation is the misuse of those powers is paradoxical but the truth remains. Henri de Lubac SJ makes the same point in a more striking way:

> Humanity is a marvel, wounded yet indestructible, which finds the meaning of its liberty in the confession of its guilt.

Just as sin inveigles its way into the warp and woof of our thoughts, words, deeds and omissions so grace comes to heal and restore us in our thoughts, words, deeds and omissions.

For a long time the sacrament of reconciliation was simply called 'confession' and many people grew up hearing statements like 'I've been to confession', 'What time are confessions?' and 'How often do you go to confession?' The act of confessing one's sins remains an essential part of the rite of the sacrament at least in its ordinary form. But the extraordinary forms of celebrating this sacrament also include confession even if only in a general way. To take part in such a celebration of reconciliation, above all by joining in a form of the *Confiteor* (I confess to Almighty God...) or in a communal act of contrition or penance, is to confess one's sinfulness before the Church. Even where a general absolution is given such a general confession is also required. The sacrament thus retains its character as an encounter between the contrite and confessing sinner and the forgiving Christ present sacramentally in this liturgy of the Church.

As already explained, in individual confession a specific statement of one's sins is required. Since the Lateran Council of 1215 Catholics who are conscious of serious sin are obliged to confess such sins each year. Even when a general absolution of sins has been received, serious sins need to be specifically confessed as soon as the person has an opportunity to celebrate the sacrament individually.

Because we are speaking about a sacrament there must be some enacted ritual - gestures, words, signs, acts and movements - that express, even to the unbelieving spectator, what is happening. Because we are speaking about a sacrament of the Church, this enactment must take a liturgical form - involving sacred places and times, persons and vestments, scripture and prayer. Together priest and penitent construct a sacramental sign of reconciliation. As a sacrament, reconciliation is related to the great sacrament of the Eucharist and as a liturgy of the Church it is related to prayer. In many situations a full liturgical celebration of the sacrament will not be possible but what the sinner provides - sins, contrition, confession - are still normally required. But it takes two to celebrate this sacrament. We must turn now to thinking about the good confessor, what it is he must do and what virtues he ought to cultivate in order to take his part in the sacramental drama.

4. THE GOOD CONFESSOR

The other party to the encounter in the sacrament of reconciliation is the priest. He too is a sinner and is not present here in a personal capacity but as one who represents Christ and the Church in this sacramental liturgy. As he prepares for the celebration of reconciliation the priest must pray for himself and for the penitents he will meet that day. He must prepare, as for other liturgies, ensuring that space, time and atmosphere are all appropriate, so that the penitent is well received and the sacrament fittingly celebrated. He must welcome the penitent and bring some light from the Word of God to the penitent as he prepares to confess his sins. He must add words of encouragement and perhaps help the penitent understand more clearly the significance and implications of his sins. He must speak the words of absolution after assigning the penitent a penance.

Tasks of the Confessor

There are two main images applied to the confessor in the Church's explanations of his role. He is a judge and he is a physician or healer. These analogies arise from the fact that the priest acts here *in persona Christi,* in the person of Christ, who although he is our Judge is also our Healer.

As a judge the confessor assists the penitent to discern and to clarify his level of responsibility as well as his understanding of what he has confessed. He must listen carefully to the confession in order to grasp the penitent's dispositions, and help the penitent to be clear about contrition including the purpose of amendment. He must also be a father in this work, anxious for the wellbeing of the penitent and keen that the penitent should see through him the just and merciful face of the Heavenly Father. He will help the penitent to see when restitution is required in order to undo the injustice resulting from his sins and will discuss with the penitent what form this ought to take.

> *The Confessor is a judge and he is a physician or healer*

As a physician or healer the confessor is to assist the penitent by prescribing some remedy for the weakness and selfishness that have led him to sin. He may well become also a teacher and spiritual guide for the penitent giving pointers about the practice of the Christian life, suggesting things the penitent might do, things he might read, and so on. The sacrament may then become a place where consciences are formed and where moral education is undertaken. The purpose of amendment - the penitent's intention not to sin again - is an important indicator of the potential for growth that is there as well as of the strength of the penitent's desire for change.

It is in the context of a sacrament that the priest thus acts as judge and physician but this does not mean that his personality and character are totally irrelevant to what is happening. It has been stressed already that this sacrament, at its heart, is a meeting between two human beings. Many of the stories one hears of people being turned off it tell of unhappy experiences of this encounter purely as a meeting between two human beings. Perhaps the priest is tired or the penitent is not as articulate as the priest would like. Perhaps one or other is hard of hearing. Perhaps the priest does not express himself clearly. Perhaps the anxieties associated with what is being done prove too much for one or other of them. Whatever the reasons there can be misunderstanding so that the penitent emerges bruised and hurt from the encounter.

John Paul II has acknowledged all this in what he says about good training for the ministry of the confessional. Such training must include what he calls 'the methodology of dialogue' (*Reconciliatio et Paenitentia*, paragraph 29). Put simply it means how to receive, listen and respond to another human being when they present themselves in the vulnerable role of the contrite and confessing sinner. It is about some basic 'human skills': how to meet, greet, receive, listen to, be with, and speak to another person. This may seem very obvious to some but it is still important to think about it because this one-to-one human conversation is the basis on which the sacrament is made just as the failure of this conversation may result in people turning away from the sacrament.

Absolution

Having listened to the penitent confess his sins, having offered his words of encouragement and advice, and having assigned an appropriate penance (see below), the priest speaks the words of absolution:

> God the Father of mercies,
> through the death and resurrection of his Son
> has reconciled the world to himself
> and sent the Holy Spirit among us
> for the forgiveness of sins;
> through the ministry of the Church
> may God give you pardon and peace,
> and I absolve you from your sins
> in the name of the Father, and of the Son, ✛
> and of the Holy Spirit.
> Amen.

Through the sacrament the fruits of Christ's paschal mystery reach the life of a particular believer. Its effects are reconciliation with God and the forgiveness of sins. The pardoned sinner lives again in grace and in peace. The 14th century German mystic Meister Eckhart says that the merit we are owed as a result of our good works, even those done while we are in the state of sin, is restored to us when we confess our sins.

The more deeply we appreciate what sin is, the more we appreciate the gift of this sacrament. If sin means alienation from God then absolution reconciles us with God. If sin means enslavement to our fallen nature then absolution frees us from that enslavement. If sin means the loss of grace then absolution means the restoration of the life of grace in us.

> *Disruption and disunity are the consequences of sin*

Sin disrupts all the relationships in which we are involved. It disrupts our relationship with God whose goodness and holiness are offended by sin. It disrupts our relationship with others who are often the direct victims of our wrongdoing but who are always affected by our sins even those that seem hidden and private. Sin disrupts our relationship with the human environment given us by God to be our garden but at odds with us now as a result of our greed (*Genesis* 3:17-19). And sin disrupts our relationship with ourselves - if we may put it like that - because the freedom we exercise in sinning is actually weakened by sin to the extent that our hearts become set on what is less than truly good.

Disruption and disunity are the consequences of sin. The sacrament brings reconciliation, restores integrity and strengthens us for the on-going battle against sin. All sin is personal in the sense of being a free act of an individual. It always has consequences for the sinner and his relationship with God. But because of our unity with others in the Body of Christ and as members of God's people, all sin has consequences for others too. We sin explicitly against our neighbour whenever we act unjustly, against his or her rights, freedom and dignity, and whenever we offend against the common good. We also sin against our neighbour through thoughts, words, deeds or omissions that express or strengthen prejudice or otherwise consolidate systems and structures of injustice in the world. Always at the heart of situations of sin, or of sinful structures, are sinful people.

All sin is a form of disobedience arising through free and conscious choice, a failure to hear and respond to the word of God's wisdom. The Bible speaks of sin also as an impersonal force that seduces and afflicts humanity. If sin is a product of human freedom it is also a power beyond the merely human, something to which other forces tempt us. For Saint Thomas Aquinas sin is evil human action, human because voluntary and evil because lacking due order. Due order in human action is assessed, he says, by human reason and by divine wisdom. He followed Saint Augustine in defining sin as a turning away from God and a turning toward the creature. He also used Augustine's other definition of sin as anything said, done, or desired contrary to the eternal law.

Together they developed the Christian understanding of sin, in particular of sin that is mortal, leading to spiritual death and the loss of eternal life (*1 John* 5:16-17).

The power of this sacrament is clear when we reflect on what it undoes and on what it makes new. Sacramental absolution refashions us in the image of Christ who is the Word

> *Sacramental absolution refashions us in the image of Christ*

and the Wisdom of God. It renews the gift of the Spirit in us so that we may be courageous workers for Christ's kingdom of love, justice and peace. It strengthens us for the on-going struggle against sin, the constant battle in which we are caught with the powers of this world. Thomas Aquinas says that to stand still on the way of the Lord is to move backwards. We must keep going, gaining freedom from the past and looking to what lies ahead (*Philippians* 3:13).

Many celebrations of the sacrament are one off encounters with an anonymous penitent in which the priest is given a snapshot or cross-section of a person's life at a particular moment. Where a person decides to confess regularly to the same priest, another kind of support and understanding becomes possible. But in every case the confessor must show sensitivity to 'the penitent's complex developing and unfinished life, with its patterns of virtue and sinfulness being redeemed by grace' (Robert Ombres OP).

Although it results from human freedom sin is also an attack on human freedom. By choosing what is less than truly good we restrict and weaken our freedom, which is our capacity for choosing the good. The confessor must help the penitent to see this and to understand the condition of his freedom. It may be that there are factors that limit the penitent's freedom and so mitigate the gravity of his sin. Grave matter alone is not sufficient for mortal sin: there must also be clear knowledge and full consent. Many factors can confuse and limit human freedom, including fear and violence. Ignorance may or may not lessen the gravity of sin depending on whether one ought to be held responsible for their ignorance or not.

Much is now known about psychological factors that can confuse desire and disturb decision-making. Some things make it difficult for people to understand what they are doing. There are some kinds of blindness for which people may not be held responsible. Other things make it difficult for people to do what is right and good even when they do succeed in understanding what they are doing. The confessor needs to develop some psychological understanding of human motivation and behaviour. Reflection on his own experience ought to be his best help in this. Many wicked things are done through ignorance and emotional reaction. The confessor needs to help the penitent to grow towards that freedom for which Christ has set us free (*Galatians* 5:1). To accept our responsibility for wrongdoing is to accept our dignity as creatures made in the image and likeness of a God who is love.

To confess sins without a purpose of amendment would make nonsense of the sacrament. How can a person be truly sorry for something they have every intention of doing again? Many of us, of course, get stuck in habits of sin of one kind or another, and can be fairly certain that we will sin again even while not wanting to. This is a different matter and is compatible with a worthy celebration of the sacrament. When it is clear that the penitent is not really sorry for their sins the priest must explain why absolution cannot then be given. It is not a question of being stingy with the grace of God. It is a matter of honesty and the mature sinner will understand this.

But the withholding of absolution is very rare and not part of the normal development of the sacramental encounter. What happens in the vast majority of cases is that an honest confession of one's sins, from a contrite heart, culminating in the act of contrition, opens the door to receiving absolution from the priest.

Penance

We have seen already that the term penance refers to a Christian virtue and that in some places and times the sacrament of reconciliation has been called simply 'the sacrament of penance'. The term is also used for the final part of the rite of reconciliation, where the priest tells the penitent to do something as a 'penance'.

Penance refers in the first place to a virtue of the Christian life, a disposition or fundamental attitude that the Christian ought to develop. The New Testament refers to this as repentance or *metanoia*, the call to turn again to Christ, to have a new mind, and to be prepared for the ongoing conversion that following Him involves. In this sense penance includes more than the sacrament of reconciliation. It takes in all the actions and processes that facilitate sanctification, moral transformation and conversion, everything that facilitates the following of Christ.

Christians sometimes referred to baptism as 'first penitence', in which they died to sin and to old sinful ways of living in order to be born to a new life. 'Second penitence' referred to everything the baptised Christian did to reinforce first penitence. It included prayer, almsgiving, fasting and other ascetical practices, any action, practice or discipline that helped the Christian to deepen and to live out their baptismal commitment.

In their efforts at conversion of life and purification of heart, Christians believed that the classical practices of prayer, fasting and almsgiving were the antidotes to the deadly sins. St Richard of Chichester, for example, wrote of this as follows:

If this book has been a blessing to you, please let me know. We'll send you our monthly *Praise News* free for one year so you can continue learning about the benefits of praising the Lord. Your name is important to us and will not be passed on to anyone else.

Merlin R. Carothers

(PLEASE PRINT IN BLOCK LETTERS)

NAME: _____

ADDRESS: _____

CITY: _____ STATE: ____ ZIP: ____

PRAISE WORKS - ALWAYS!

FOUNDATION OF PRAISE
PO BOX 2518
ESCONDIDO CA 92033-2518

Satisfaction consists in the cutting off of the causes of the sin. Thus, fasting is the proper antidote to lust; prayer to pride, to envy, anger and sloth; alms to covetousness.

The Church's liturgical celebrations of penance build on these practices of the virtue of penance and include non-sacramental penitential liturgies as well as the sacrament of reconciliation itself. If the celebration of the sacrament is to be renewed then perhaps a key factor will be recovering a sense of the sacrament as the culmination of this process. The sacrament focuses, celebrates and makes real in people's lives something essential to Christian life. It makes visible spiritual realities that are permanent and on-going (see *Reconciliatio et Paenitentia* paragraph 4).

Interior and External Penance

Within the sacrament itself a distinction was sometimes made, between 'interior penance' - meaning contrition, justification, repentance and conversion - and 'external penance' - meaning the sacramental rite itself, the actual confession of one's sins to a priest, the priest's words and gestures, and the 'satisfaction' or particular penance that completed the sacrament.

St Richard of Chichester referred to penance as satisfaction and this is a term that is still used in relation to the penance given to the penitent by the confessor.

The desire to make satisfaction for one's sins is part of genuine contrition. To be genuinely sorry for sin will include the desire to undo its consequences (to the extent that this might be possible) and to set right the order of justice that has been disturbed. In some cases restitution - paying back what has been stolen, for example - will be necessary.

But even where restitution is not possible, and what has been done cannot be undone, the penitent is still given a penance. The penance has a number of functions. It retains something of the character of a tariff. We saw that this idea originated with the penitential books of the Celtic church. Although sometimes compared with the punishment imposed by a judge, its purpose is more positive than that. The rite says that it is intended 'as a remedy for sin and a help to renewal of life' (*Rite of Penance*, paragraph 6c). So the penance is a kind of medicine because this is a sacrament of spiritual healing and the priest who represents Christ our Healer must help the penitent to counter the temptations of sin with the discipline and practices of Christian living.

If the penance is a way of re-enforcing the reality of sin and its consequences, it is also a way of re-enforcing and expressing the contrition of the penitent. It is the clearest sign of the penitent's purpose of amendment and shows that he is serious in his intention not to sin again. Very often penance takes the form of prayers to be said.

This is to strengthen the penitent's relationship with God from whom alone we receive the grace to avoid sin.

It is important to stress that the saying or doing of the penance is still part of the sacramental liturgy. It is not that one says or does one's penance after the celebration of reconciliation. The penance is the final moment in the liturgical celebration. Significantly it is normally when the penitent has returned either to the main body of the church or to his everyday life that he fulfils the penance assigned to him.

It is as if the penitent returns to the world with a mission. From the earliest times the rite of reconciliation included the laying on of hands by the bishop or priest on the head of the penitent. It survives in the present rite although often now attenuated to the priest raising his hand in blessing as he says the words of absolution. But it was part of the ancient rite. Indeed Karl Rahner SJ says that the imposition of hands was the final moment in the entire penitential process in the early Church (*Theological Investigations* 15, pages 156-71, page 234).

The laying on of hands is a very ancient and significant gesture in the sacramental life of the Church. It is an epiclesis, a calling down of the Spirit on a Christian who is being commissioned or deputed, called out from the community for a particular task. It is always associated with a task or mission on behalf of the Church for which a special gift of the Spirit is required. We read of it in Acts

6:6 where the first deacons are ordained. In Acts 8:17 baptised Christians receive the Holy Spirit when Peter and John lay their hands on them. When Paul and Barnabas are 'set apart' at Antioch the leaders of the Church there laid their hands on them as they sent them off to preach, the work to which the Spirit had called them (*Acts* 13:3). The apostles are told by Jesus that they will lay their hands on the sick who will recover (*Mark* 16:18).

The imposition of hands is still part of the sacraments of ordination, anointing and reconciliation. If the sinner is one of those sick people who is healed through the prayers and ministry of the apostles, he is also a Christian designated for a particular work in the Church. He bears witness to the grace and mercy of God. He has become an ambassador for Christ (*2 Corinthians* 5:20) who, because he has been forgiven much, ought also now to love much (*Luke* 7:47).

Forgive as you have been forgiven

In chapter 7 of the Gospel of Luke we hear about a sinful woman who washed the feet of Jesus in the house of a Pharisee. The story reaches its climax with Jesus saying that...

> ...her sins, which are many, have been forgiven; hence she has shown great love. But the one to whom little is forgiven, loves little (Luke 7:47, Revised Standard Version).

The Jerusalem Bible translation reads:

> ...her sins, her many sins, must have been forgiven her,
> or she would not have shown such great love. It is the
> man who is forgiven little who shows little love.

The New American Version reads it differently:

> ...that is why her many sins are forgiven - because of her
> great love. Little is forgiven the one whose love is small.

And yet another translation has it this way:

> ...her sins which are many are forgiven for she loved
> much; but he who is forgiven little, loves little (Nestle-
> Aland, Stuttgart 1992).

A note in the Jerusalem Bible accepts that the Nestle-Aland translation is more accurate to the text but that the RSV and its own translation is more accurate to the context.

Did this woman love much because her sins had been forgiven or were her sins forgiven because she loved much? How are we to understand the cause of forgiveness? In the Middle Ages there was a disagreement between theologians who thought contrition was the cause of forgiveness (Peter Abelard and Peter Lombard) and theologians who thought absolution was its cause (Richard and Hugh of the school of Saint Victor). Thomas Aquinas, as so often, combines these answers, saying that the sacramental exchange involves material and formal causes, the first being contrition and the second absolution.

If we stay with Thomas Aquinas we will say that all is God's grace and that we can do nothing without God. Without grace we cannot repent. But this does not exclude human freedom without which we could not sin and without which we could not respond to the call to repentance. God and the human being are not rival powers within some system of forces. God's grace works within us in a way that is completely respectful of human freedom. Saint Thomas presents the idea most bluntly when he says that God's Spirit 'makes us do freely' what is good.

It is mysterious, the link between love and forgiveness in Luke 7:47 as the different translations testify, and we might well want things to be clearer. But perhaps the lack of simple clarity is more true to our experience of how God and the human being are involved with each other. On one side we know it is wrong to think that we earn God's forgiveness through the quality of our contrition. On the other we know it is wrong to think that what we do is irrelevant to our standing with God.

What is clearer, though, is that we ought to forgive others as we have ourselves been forgiven. We are ambassadors of reconciliation not only in telling others of the reconciliation won by Christ but in working for reconciliation wherever we can and in trying to build it wherever we can. Jesus reminds us about the connection between the forgiveness we have received and the forgiveness we ought to give (*Matthew* 6:12-15).

We assume that a person who has experienced a difficulty will be sympathetic to another person faced with the same or a similar difficulty. But the parable of the wicked servant teaches us that this is not necessarily so (*Matthew* 18:32). The servant seems to forget very quickly how much he had himself been forgiven. Once again it is important that we remember, remember more and remember better, remember above all how we have been forgiven by God. Remembering this ought to equip us to forgive. It ought to help us find our way through the obstacles there undoubtedly are to forgiving others. It may also be, of course, that the one we find difficult to forgive is God.

As the Word of the Father, Jesus knows all. He knows what is in human hearts (*John* 2:24-25) and he knows what is in God's heart (*John* 1:18). He identified so completely with our sinful situation that Saint Paul speaks of him 'being made to be sin who knew no sin' (*2 Corinthians* 5:21). He humbled himself even to death on a cross (*Philippians* 2:8), a death we believe to be for the forgiveness of sins. He descended to the spirits in prison and led them forth into the freedom of God's kingdom (*1 Peter* 3:19), making captivity itself a captive when he ascended on high (*Ephesians* 4:8) with all angels, authorities and powers made subject to him (*1 Peter* 3:22). He now holds the keys of Death and of Hell (*Revelation* 1:18).

The One who understands all because he is the Word remembers all and to him is given all authority to forgive sins. He shares in the Father's power and he shares this power and authority with his body, the Church. He is the Forgiver of all and it is He who gives us the forgiveness with which we may forgive others just as it is He who gives us the love with which we may love others.

One of the forms of dismissal at the end of the celebration of reconciliation puts it neatly:

> Go in peace,
> and proclaim to the world
> the wonderful works of God,
> who has brought you salvation.

5. Some Saints on the Sacrament of Reconciliation

The understanding of the saints in relation to sin is encouraging, particularly if we are tempted to become depressed at the thought of our sinfulness. St John Climacus wrote that no one really wants to sin against God and yet we do all sin without being forced to do so. St Gregory Nazianzen agrees. To do no wrong is supernatural, he says, and belongs to God alone.

Not that the saints regarded sinning as something unimportant: on the contrary they are very clear that it means the death of the soul, the loss of grace and alienation from God. St Paul of the Cross gives the following advice:

> Should we fall into sin, let us at once humble ourselves sorrowfully in His presence, and then, with an act of unbounded confidence, let us throw ourselves into the ocean of His goodness, where every failing will be cancelled and anxiety will be turned into love.

Saint Therese of Lisieux, now a Doctor of the Church, teaches the same:

> If my conscience were burdened with all the sins it is possible to commit, I would still go and throw myself into our Lord s arms, my heart all broken up with contrition.

I know what tenderness He has for any prodigal child of His that comes back to Him.

It is by comparison with the love of God that we realise the sadness of our sins even though there is never any common measure between our fault and God's mercy. St Francis de Sales, one of the gentlest of the saints, writes about this as follows:

Who will dare to measure, by the greatness of his sins, the immensity of that infinite mercy which casts them all into the depths of the sea of oblivion, when we repent of them with love?

The saints have always valued the sacrament of reconciliation and made frequent use of it themselves. St Isidore of Seville writes about the importance of the sacrament which he refers to simply as 'confession':

Confession heals, confession justifies, confession grants pardon of sin. All hope consists in confession. In confession there is a chance for mercy. Believe it firmly. Do not doubt, do not hesitate, never despair of the mercy of God. Hope and have confidence in confession.

FURTHER READING

On the Sacraments:

Baptism (CTS Publications, 2004; Do 712).
Confirmation (CTS Publications, 2004; Do 713).
Eucharist (CTS Publications, 2004; Do 714).
Reconciliation (CTS Publications, 2004; Do 716).
Anointing (CTS Publications, 2004; Do 711).
Marriage (CTS Publications, 2004; Do 710).
Holy Orders (CTS Publications, 2004; Do 715).

Liturgical Texts

Sacred Congregation for Divine Worship, *Introduction to the Rite of Penance* 1974 [found also in Crichton below]
J.D. Crichton, *The Ministry of Reconciliation. A Commentary on the Order of Penance 1974*, Chapman, London 1974

Vatican Documents

Catechism of the Catholic Church paragraphs 1422-1498
John Paul II, *Reconciliatio et Paenitentia. Post-Synodal Apostolic Exhortation on Reconciliation and Penance in the Mission of the Church Today* 1984
John Paul II, *Veritatis Splendor. Encyclical Letter Regarding Certain Fundamental Questions of the Church's Moral Teaching* 1993
John Paul II, *Misericordia Dei. Apostolic Letter Motu Priorio on Certain Aspects of the Celebration of the Sacrament of Penance* 2002

Lumen Gentium paragraph 11
Sacrosanctum Concilium paragraphs 72-75

Other Reading

Martha Alken OP, *The Healing Power of Forgiving* Crossroad Publishing, New York 1997

Paul Anciaux, *The Sacrament of Penance* Challoner Publications, London 1962

Chris Aridas, *Reconciliation*: Celebrating God's Healing Forgiveness Image Books, Doubleday, New York 1987

John M.T. Barton, *Penance and Absolution* Burns and Oates, London 1961

Philippe Bequerie and Claude Duchesneau, *How to Understand the Sacraments* SCM London 1991

Francis J.Buckley *'I Confess': The Sacrament of Penance Today* Ave Maria Press, Notre Dame, Indiana 1972

Hugh Connolly, *Sin* New Century Theology, Continuum, London and New York 2002

Henri de Lubac SJ, *A Brief Catechesis on Nature and Grace* Ignatius Press, San Francisco 1984

Sean Fagan SM, *Has Sin Changed? A Book on Forgiveness* Gill and Macmillan, Dublin 1988

John Fitzsimons, editor *Penance: Virtue and Sacrament* Burns and Oates, London 1969

Bernard Häring CSsR, *Shalom: Peace. The Sacrament of Reconciliation* Image Books, Doubleday, New York 1969

Bernard Häring CSsR, *The Sacrament of Reconciliation* St Paul Publications 1980

F.J. Heggen *Confession and the Service of Penance* Sheed and Ward, London 1967

Monika K. Hellwig *Sign of Reconciliation and Conversion: The Sacrament of Penance For Our Times* Michael Glazier, Wilmington, Delaware 1984

L. Gregory Jones, *Embodying Forgiveness. A Theological Analysis* Eerdmans Publishing, Grand Rapids, Michigan 1995

John Mahoney, 'The Influence of Auricular Confession', in *The Making of Moral Theology* Clarendon Press, Oxford 1987

Phelim McGowan and Flor McCarthy SDB, *Welcome Home. A Prayerful Reflection on the Sacrament of Reconciliation* Dominican Publications, Dublin 1998

R.C. Mortimer, *The Origins of Private Penace in the Western Church* Oxford 1939

New Catholic Encyclopedia Confession: 4.131-37, 142-45; 16.94-95; 17.151; Penance: 11.72-84, 84-88; 16.335-37; 17.497-501; Reconciliation: 12.129-30; 17.554-56

Henry Nouwen, *The Return of the Prodigal Son: A Story of Homecoming* Darton, Longman and Todd, London 1992

Ladislas Orsy SJ, *The Evolving Church and the Sacrament of Penance* Dimension Books, Denville NJ 1978

Eugene O Sullivan OP, *Celebrating Reconciliation* Zealandia, Auckland 1982

Karl Rahner SJ, *Theological Investigations. Volume 15*: *Penance in the Early Church* Darton, Longman and Todd, London 1983

J. Randolph *Confession* Ignatius Press, San Francisco 2001

Max Thurian, *Confession* Mowbray, London and Oxford 1985

Adrienne von Speyr, *Confession* Ignatius Press, San Francisco 1985

Informative Catholic Reading

We hope that you have enjoyed reading this booklet.

If you would like to find out more about CTS booklets - we'll send you our free information pack and catalogue.

Please send us your details:

Name ....

Address ....

....

....

Postcode ....

Telephone..

Email ....

Send to: CTS, 40-46 Harleyford Road,
             Vauxhall, London
             SE11 5AY

Tel: 020 7640 0042
Fax: 020 7640 0046
Email: info@cts-online.org.uk